SHIRLEY CHISHOLM DARED

THE STORY OF THE
FIRST BLACK WOMAN IN CONGRESS

————————

WRITTEN BY ALICIA D. WILLIAMS
ILLUSTRATED BY APRIL HARRISON

For Nailah.
Always dare to be yourself.
—A.D.W.

This is dedicated to all the God-fearing, daring women, both past and present, who were and are still a part of my life. Lucy, my mother, a strict disciplinarian, a daring and determined spirit who possessed an infallible love. My sisters, Jamell and Barbara, who show love, keep it real, balance me out, and make sure I stay the course. My "girlfriends"—my constructive critics, cheerleaders, and soundboards. I thank God for each one of you. With all my love. —A.H.

A note about the illustrations: Shirley traveled to Barbados aboard the *Vulcania*, and the flag pictured is from that ship.

Photo of Shirley Chisholm announcing her candidacy for presidency: Library of Congress, Prints & Photographs Division, *U.S. News & World Report Magazine Collection*, LC-DIG-ppmsca-55937.

The text of this book is set in 16.25-point Adobe Caslon Pro Semibold.
The illustrations were rendered in acrylic and mixed media collage.
Book design by Rachael Cole.

Text copyright © 2021 by Alicia D. Williams.
Illustrations copyright © 2021 by April Harrison.
All rights reserved. Published by Scholastic Inc., 557 Broadway, New York, NY 10012, by arrangement with Random House Children's Books, a division of Penguin Random House LLC.
Printed in the U.S.A.

ISBN 978-1-338-85768-9

5 6 7 8 9 10   40   31 30 29 28 27 26 25 24 23

Scholastic Inc., 557 Broadway, New York, NY 10012

SHIRLEY CHISHOLM DARED

THE STORY OF THE
FIRST BLACK WOMAN IN CONGRESS

WRITTEN BY **ALICIA D. WILLIAMS**
ILLUSTRATED BY **APRIL HARRISON**

SCHOLASTIC INC.

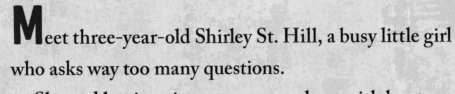

Meet three-year-old Shirley St. Hill, a busy little girl who asks way too many questions.

She and her immigrant parents, along with her two baby sisters, live in a tiny apartment in Brooklyn—one they can hardly afford.

Seeing that Shirley needs room to run, her mother thinks it might be a good idea to take her to her grandma's. Plus they'll save money.

So the girls and their mother board an ol' steamship
in New York Harbor and set off for Barbados.

After nine days, the family arrives to welcoming hugs and kisses.

But just as the island's smells and sounds start to feel
familiar to Shirley, it's time for Mother to say goodbye.

Still, Shirley doesn't settle into sadness, oh no. She has work to do. Though she's younger and tinier than her cousins, she's just as strong. She hauls buckets of well water to thirsty cows, pigs, and goats. Shirley even bosses her cousins around!

7

When classes start in the British one-room schoolhouse, four-year-old Shirley proudly sits on the front bench. And won't budge.

That girl is daring!

Back in the States, the Great Depression begins. Many people lose their jobs and can't afford homes or food.

Mother makes little as a seamstress and Father as a baker's helper.

10

But they miss their daughters' laughter bouncing off the
walls so much that after six years, they bring the girls home.
Shirley moves back to Brooklyn.

11

At P.S. 84, the principal introduces Shirley to her new classroom. Third grade?!

Hasn't she already learned third-grade reading, writing, and arithmetic? Sure, she's only nine years old—but in Barbados she had just been promoted to sixth grade!

Sorry, but you don't know American social studies or geography, the principal tells her.

Hmph. In no time, Shirley is bored . . . and restless.

She snaps rubber bands at kids' heads. She flicks spitballs when the teacher turns her back.

Finally, *finally*, the school assigns her an American history tutor. And just over a year later, Shirley proudly sits in the eighth grade.

Every day over dinner, her father asks what she's learned. Every day Shirley offers details. And every day he tells her, "Study and make something of yourself."

In the evenings, Shirley listens in as her father and his friends discuss politics—how poor people are being mistreated and that folks should fight for their rights. She learns about a man named W. E. B. Du Bois, who spoke of Negro rights, and Marcus Garvey, who spoke of Black pride.

By the time Shirley
begins Girls High School,
her mother is warning:
Come straight home.
Focus on your homework
and piano practice. No
pop music! Absolutely
no boys!

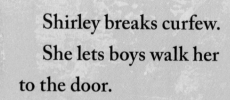

Shirley breaks curfew.
She lets boys walk her
to the door.
And instead of classical
music, she plays jazz.

16

That young lady is rebellious!

Mother tries to explain that she's strict because she wants Shirley to grow up and *be* someone.

Now meet seventeen-year-old Shirley, a smart young lady who attends Brooklyn College. She studies sociology and Spanish—it isn't acceptable for Black women to study politics or law. But that doesn't stop her from joining the Political Science Society.

Political Science Meeting

After graduation, Shirley tries to get a job as a teacher, but over and over, she is told she doesn't look old enough. She finally exclaims to a nursery school director, "Give me a chance to find out whether I can do the job!"

That woman is persistent!

And on the spot, the director of Mount Calvary Child Care Center hires Shirley as a teacher's aide.

After work, Shirley travels more than an hour by subway to take classes at Columbia University Teachers College.

She attends political meetings, too. When she has a question, Shirley bravely thrusts her hand into the air. She asks:

Where's the money to make schools better in her Bedford-Stuyvesant community?

Why isn't trash picked up regularly?

Why can't Bed-Stuy have as much police protection as other districts?

That woman is **too** *persistent!*

21

Politicians promise to help. But don't.

So Shirley joins the Seventeenth Assembly District Democratic Club—during a time when women members can only do chores like writing thank-you cards. Each year, the club holds a banquet to raise money, and the donations are collected in cigar boxes. Shirley's role: cigar-box decorator. She paints, glues pictures, and makes the boxes so dazzling that people can't help but give.

Still, Shirley wants to know:

Why are only women making cards and decorating boxes?

Why should we put up with this?

Yeah, echo the other women, why *should* we put up with this?

That Shirley is a troublemaker!

Finally, the club sends a letter thanking Shirley for her hard work—and kicking her out.

Shirley isn't bothered. After all, people don't have to be members to attend meetings, or to ask questions.

When she is twenty-five years old, Shirley St. Hill
marries her college sweetheart, Conrad Chisholm.

Meet Shirley Chisholm, a busy young woman who still asks way too many questions. Teaching now takes over her life. At twenty-nine, she becomes director of the Friend in Need Nursery school, and a year later, director of the Hamilton-Madison Child Care Center.

In her community, politicians keep making promises.
Yet nothing changes.

So Shirley steps her white oxford heels back into politics.
She helps create the Unity Democratic Club. She works to
organize after-school programs for kids and improve housing
conditions for inner-city neighborhoods. She organizes
voters, stuffs envelopes, and circulates petitions.

A seat in the New York State Assembly opens—but there's one problem: it has always, *always* been made up of daring, rebellious, persistent *white men*. Shirley isn't deterred.

During the campaign, words, words, and more words are thrown at her.

HAVE YOU COOKED YOUR HUSBAND'S BREAKFAST YET?

SHOULDN'T YOU BE CLEANING YOUR HOUSE?

WOMEN OUGHT TO TAKE CARE OF THEIR FAMILIES, NOT RUN FOR OFFICE!

Shirley hears only the most important words, from her father long ago: *Make something of yourself.*

Election night, 1964. The votes are tallied:
18,149 . . . 18,150 . . . 18,151 . . .
20,957 votes have been cast—and Shirley
Chisholm wins by more than 16,000!

Over the next three years, Shirley introduces bills to help disadvantaged students pay for college and to give unemployment insurance to domestic workers.

She speaks up so much that assemblymen complain. When she refuses to follow their rules, they call her a bossy troublemaker. When she challenges them, they mutter that she doesn't belong. What does Shirley do?

She runs for Congress!

She posts signs and hands out flyers, talks to ladies sitting on park benches and men standing on street corners, visits housing projects, churches, and living rooms, too. She works and works and works.

Her campaign slogan is: "Unbought and Unbossed!"

35

Her fellow assemblymen refuse to support her. Even reporters ignore her, only interviewing her opponent.

Shirley protests.

"Who are you?" they retort. "Just a little schoolteacher who *happened* to go to the Assembly."

Hasn't Shirley helped students pay for college? Hasn't she proposed bills to fund day care centers? Hasn't she organized rallies, driven voters to the polls, and fought for the rights of the poor?

But could she—dare she—win?

" I am and always will be a catalyst for change. "

Election night, 1968. The votes are tallied:

34,883 . . . 34,884 . . . 34,885 . . .

52,433 votes are cast—Shirley Chisholm wins by more than 21,000 votes!

This—

JET

November 3, 1968

First Black Woman IN U.S. Cong

Shirley Chisholm

"If they don't give you a seat at the table, bring a folding chair."

OAKLAND POST

Shirley Chisholm

Congresswoman Shirley Chisholm . . .

First Negro Woman Wins Seat in U.S. Congress

Shirley Chisholm 3 - Newspap

Mrs. Shirley Chisholm: Political Trail Blazer

Daring!
Rebellious!
Persistent!
Troublemaker!—
is the *first* African American woman elected to Congress!
(And she never stops asking questions.)

AUTHOR'S NOTE

How did Shirley Chisholm become so bossy, bold, and daring? Perhaps it was due to lessons learned from Grandmother Seale while living in Barbados. Or from listening to her father passionately debate with friends. Or maybe she was simply born gutsy.

Shirley's West Indian parents, Ruby Seale and Charles St. Hill, met in Brooklyn, New York, and married. Their sweet Shirley was born on November 30, 1924. Like many immigrants, they struggled financially and eventually sent Shirley and her sisters, Odessa and Muriel, to Barbados. They would later have another daughter, Selma.

There's a sense of pride in the Barbadian people that Shirley took to. Although descendants of enslaved people, Barbadians were never made to feel inferior to whites.

Shirley's early schooling was very strict. Teachers expected students to pay close attention—or get a whipping. Even at age four, Shirley suffered her fair share of whippings! From then on, she always took her education seriously.

From 1942 to 1946, Shirley attended Brooklyn College. She became active in the Harriet Tubman Society, the NAACP, and the Urban League and helped form Ipothia (In Pursuit of the Highest in All), a society of Black women students.

At Columbia University's Teachers College, she met Conrad Chisholm. They married in 1949, but though he fully supported Shirley's political passion, they divorced in 1977. Shirley later married New York State legislator Arthur Hardwick, Jr.

Congresswoman Shirley Chisholm announcing her candidacy for the presidential nomination

In 1968, during her run for Congress, Shirley became ill. Just days after having a noncancerous tumor removed, she willed herself back onto the campaign trail, announcing: "This is Fighting Shirley Chisholm and I'm up and around. . . ." Shirley beat Republican and civil rights activist James Farmer, then hired mainly women—both Black and white—as her staff.

Shirley helped found several political organizations, including the Congressional Black Caucus, the National Women's Political Caucus, and the Congressional Women's Caucus.

On January 25, 1972, Shirley announced her candidacy for the Democratic nomination for president. She made history as the *first* African American woman to do so. Although she did not win, Shirley remained in Congress for eleven more years. In 1983, she retired from office, then taught at Mount Holyoke College until 1987.

After suffering a series of strokes, Shirley Chisholm died on January 1, 2005, at the age of eighty.

Shirley worked tirelessly *fighting* for the rights of underrepresented people. I like to think that she also opened the doors for *everyone* to speak up for the voiceless, challenge a political system that has been too long run by old white men, and press on against all odds. And I hope that she dares each and every one of us to be brave, just as she was.

ALICIA D. WILLIAMS dares to be herself, just as Shirley Chisholm wished for everyone. She received a Newbery Honor and the Coretta Scott King–John Steptoe New Talent Author Award for her debut middle-grade novel, *Genesis Begins Again.* In addition, the book was a Kirkus Prize nominee and a William C. Morris Award finalist. She is also an oral storyteller in the African American tradition. Alicia is a Master Teaching Artist and infuses her love for drama and writing to teach arts integration. She sips her coffee while writing her stories in Charlotte, North Carolina.

APRIL HARRISON has a clear-eyed artistic vision and never shies away from a creative challenge. Like Shirley, she dares! April won the Coretta Scott King–John Steptoe New Talent Illustrator Award for Patricia C. McKissack's final picture book, *What Is Given from the Heart.* The book received four starred reviews and was hailed in a review by the *New York Times* as an "exquisite story of generosity." Most recently, she illustrated *Nana Akua Goes to School* by Tricia Elam Walker, which also received four starred reviews. A renowned folk artist, April lives in Greenville, South Carolina.